Look What You Can Make With

Plastic Bottles and Tubs

Edited by Kathy Ross
Photographs by Hank Schneider

Boyds Mills Press

Craft Coordinator:

Kathy Ross

Craft Makers:

Kerry O'Neill
Kathy Ross

Contributors:

Dorothy F. Appleton
Katherine Corliss Bartow
Dorris Caines
Jennifer Carling
Barbara Casper
Marie E. Cecchini
Rosie Centrone
Mindy Cherez
Kent Douglas
Paige Matthews Eckard
Laurie Edwards
JoAnn Fluegeman
Mary Galligan

Norah Grubmeyer
Edna Harrington
Joann M. Hart
Murley Kay Kight
Karen Kremsreiter
Lory MacRae
Judy Manchanda
Carol McCall
Donna Miers
Clare Mishica
June Rose Mobly
Sandra J. Noll
James W. Perrin, Jr.

Jane K. Priewe
Kathy Ross
Andrew Smith
Matthew Stockton
Marilyn Thomason
Sharon Dunn Umnik
S. Uslan
Jan J. Van Pelt
Frances Wales
Dava Walker
D. A. Woodliff
Mildred K. Zibulka
Patsy N. Zimmerman

Published by Bell Books
Boyds Mills Press, Inc.
A Highlights Company
815 Church Street
Honesdale, Pennsylvania 18431
Printed in China

U.S. Cataloging-in-Publication Data
  (Library of Congress Standards)

Look what you can make with plastic bottles and tubs : over 80 pictured crafts
and dozens of other ideas / edited by Kathy Ross ; photographs by Hank
Schneider. — 1st ed.
[48] p. : col. photos. ; cm.
Includes index.
Summary: Toys, games, and other things to make from plastic bottles and tubs.
ISBN: 1-56397-567-X
1. Plastic bottle craft — Juvenile literature. 2. Plastics craft — Juvenile
literature . [1. Plastic bottle craft. 2. Plastics craft .] I. Schneider,
Hank. II. Title.
745.572 21 2001 AC CIP
2001091961

First edition, 2001
Books in this series originally designed by Lorianne Siomades
The text of this book is set in 10-point Avant Garde Demi, titles 43-point Gill Sans Extra Bold

Visit our Web site at www.boydsmillspress.com

10 9 8 7 6 5 4 3 2

Getting Started

This book is filled with fun, easy-to-make crafts, and each one begins with a plastic bottle or tub. You'll find a wide variety of things to make, including toys, games, and gifts.

Directions

Before you start each craft, read the directions and look closely at the photograph, but remember—it's up to you to make the craft your own. If we decorate a craft with markers but you want to use glitter paint and stickers, go for it. Feel free to stray from our directions and invent new crafts.

Work Area

It's a good idea to keep your work area covered. Old newspapers, brown paper (from grocery bags), or old sheets work well. Also, protect your clothes by wearing a smock. A big old shirt does the job and gives you room to move. Finally, remember to clean up when you've finished.

Materials

You'll need a lot of plastic bottles and containers, so start saving now. Ask friends and relatives to help. Keep your craft-making supplies together, and before making each craft, check the "You Will Need" list to make sure you have everything. In this list we will often specify a certain type of container. For some crafts, however, more than one kind of container will work. Look at the type of container used for the craft pictured, then see what you might have on hand that is similar in shape and size. Also, since you'll need scissors, glue, tape, or a stapler for almost every craft, we don't list these supplies.

Other Stuff

When we show several similar crafts, we'll often list numbered directions that apply to all of the crafts, then specific directions for each craft. When you start a craft, make sure the bottle or container is clean and the label has been removed, if possible. Warm, soapy water is helpful in loosening labels. Sometimes you will need adult help scraping off a label and the glue that might be left behind. Every once in a while we come across a label that will not come off. In this case we use the container for a project that allows you to cover the label, rather than remove it.

Some containers are easier to cut than others. Soaking a container in warm water will soften it and make cutting easier. If you are having trouble cutting a container, ask for adult help.

Several of the projects call for paint. Because the bottles and tubs are plastic, poster paint is not the best choice. The best paint for these projects is a non-toxic acrylic paint. This is readily available in craft stores.

That's about all. So, choose a craft and check your container stash for just the right one for the job, and have fun. Before you know it, you'll be showing everyone what you made with plastic bottles and tubs.

Bottle Town

Turn bottles into an entire neighborhood.

You Will Need:

- plastic bottles
- construction paper
- markers
- craft beads, rickrack, sequins, pompons, craft feathers, yarn
- poster board
- hole punch
- metal paper fasteners
- cotton balls
- tops from old lipstick or glue-stick tubes
- lids and caps
- small plastic pill bottles
- masking tape

To Make the Houses

Cut around each bottle about 3 to 5 inches from the bottom. The bottom of the bottle will become the house. Cut doors and windows from paper, and glue them to the house. Add details with markers, beads, and other trims. Fold a piece of poster board in half, and cut a roof for the house. Punch a hole in the back top edge of the house and in the back center of the roof. Attach the roof to the house with a paper fastener so that the roof will open. Use cut paper and other decorations to add details to the roof, such as a chimney. Glue a puff of cotton to the top of the chimney for smoke.

To Make the Tube Puppets

Snip some fuzz off the side of a pompon for colorful hair. Glue the hair to the top of the tube. Punch eyes from paper. Add pupils with a marker. Glue the eyes to the tube. Glue a tiny pompon to the tube for a nose. Add other trims. Slip the tubes over your fingers to use as fingerpuppets.

To Make the Lid People

Glue a variety of lids and caps together to create a person. Add details with ribbon, buttons, and other items.

To Make the Pill-Bottle Pals

To make people, cover the top part of the bottle with two rows of masking tape for the head. Color the tape with markers, and draw on a face. Add yarn hair. You might want to add hair ribbons to make a girl. Wrap the bottom half of the bottle in construction paper for the clothes. Trim with rickrack or other decorations.

For an animal, leave the bottle uncovered, or wrap in construction paper. Add details using markers and trims. Stuff the inside of the bottle with cotton balls to give the puppet a snug fit on your finger.

More Ideas

Use bottles of different colors and sizes to make a whole neighborhood of houses. How about an apartment building made from a tall bottle? You might want to add a fire station made from a large red detergent bottle. You really should have a library! What else?

Glue lids on the people for hats. Try using wiggle eyes, trims, tiny beads, and buttons for your tube puppets. Let your imagination take over, and make your people as varied and interesting as real people.

For animals, tip the bottles sideways and use the bottoms for the faces.

Comet Toy

Make this comet for some outdoor fun.

You Will Need:

- round plastic bottle with cap
- colored tissue paper
- colored plastic tape

1 Cut the top part off the bottle for the nose of the comet. Leave the cap on the bottle.

2 Cut long strips of colorful tissue paper for the tail.

3 Glue the ends of the tissue-paper strips around the inside of the bottle. Let the glue dry.

4 Decorate the outside of the bottle with strips of colored plastic tape. Toss the comet into the air, and watch the flowing tail follow as it falls.

More Ideas

Make one for Independence Day with red, white, and blue streamers.

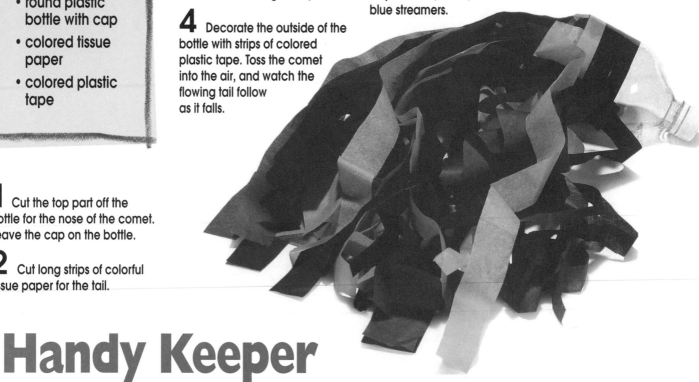

Handy Keeper

Here's a fancy container for storing tiny items.

You Will Need:

- container with plastic lid
- wallpaper scrap
- old greeting card picture
- permanent marker

1 Cover the container with wallpaper.

2 Cut a picture from an old greeting card. Glue the picture to the side of the container.

3 Label the top with the name of what you plan to store in it.

More Ideas

Make a matching set of two or three containers for your mom or dad to store nuts and bolts, sugar packets, or small treasures.

Clowning Around

Use these puppets to put on a show.

You Will Need:

- plastic dish-soap bottles
- medium-size plastic-foam ball
- foot-long stick or dowel
- fabric
- two wooden beads
- felt, pompons, yarn, ribbon, chenille sticks
- aluminum foil
- colored tissue paper
- rubber band
- cotton

More Ideas

Cut out white-felt wings to make an angel puppet.

To Make Clonker Clown

Cut the bottom from the plastic bottle. Push the plastic-foam ball onto one end of the dowel, and glue it in place. Put the end of the dowel down through the neck of the bottle. Press and twist the ball onto the bottleneck. Glue the head in place and let dry. Cut two strips of fabric for arms. Tie a wooden bead to each strip. Glue the end of each arm on each side of the top of the bottle. Use the felt and other trims to give the clown a face, hair, and clothes. When you hold the clown puppet by the dowel and twirl it back and forth, the hands will "clonk" against the bottle.

To Make the Clown Stick Puppet

Turn the bottle upside down so that the bottom of the bottle becomes the top of the clown head. Cover foil with a thin layer of glue, then with a sheet of tissue paper. Shape the foil, tissue-side out, over the head. Secure the hat with a rubber band at the bottom where you wish the brim to be. Turn the foil out below the rubber band to make the brim. Trim off the excess foil. Decorate the hat. Add details for a face. Glue a funny fabric bow at the neck. To make the handle, soak a wad of cotton in a mixture of glue and water. Wrap enough cotton around the stick so that it will fit snugly in the spout.

Vases and Planters with Pizzazz

Hold your flowers and houseplants in these unique containers.

You Will Need:

- various plastic bottles and tubs
- fabric
- pencil
- ruler
- ribbon, yarn, and trims
- paper plate
- rubber band
- chenille sticks
- food coloring
- toothpicks

To Make the Fabric-Covered Planter

Place a tub on the wrong side of a large piece of fabric. Trace around the tub. Measure the height of the tub and add 2 inches. Enlarge the circle by that amount all the way around, and cut the circle out. Rub glue around the inside rim of the tub. Set the tub on the center of the circle, and fold the fabric up, pressing the edges into the glue. Place another tub inside the first tub. Tie a ribbon around the rim.

To Make the Yarn-Covered Planter

Cover the outside of a plastic container with glue. Starting at the bottom, wrap the container with bands of different-colored yarns. Glue a simple shape made from yarn onto the planter.

To Make the Fluted Flower Basket

Glue the bottom of a small round tub to the center of a paper plate. Let the glue dry. Cut flaps every 2 to 3 inches from the outer edge of the plate to the bottom of the container. Glue the flaps in place around the container. A rubber band will help secure them while the glue dries. Remove the rubber band when the glue has dried, and tie a pretty ribbon around the container. Punch a hole on either side of the container. Twist two chenille sticks together to make a handle. Insert each end into a hole, and twist the ends to secure.

To Make the Painted Vase

In separate containers, mix a tiny drop of food coloring with a small amount of white glue. Use a different toothpick as a paintbrush for each color. Dot around the top and bottom of a clear plastic jar with the colored glues. (Use tiny amounts of colored glue, or it will run down the side.) Draw a simple design around the vase. Tie a pretty ribbon around the rim.

More Ideas

Instead of painting the vase, cover it with glue, then sprinkle with glitter.

Shipshape Vessels

Launch these boats in your sink or bathtub.

You Will Need:

- plastic detergent bottle
- white construction paper
- clear packing tape
- plastic drinking straw
- modeling clay
- permanent markers
- white dish-soap bottle
- hole punch
- toothpaste cap
- paint and paintbrush
- plastic berry basket
- plastic scraps
- dowel

More Ideas

Make passengers for the ships by drawing faces with a permanent marker on something that floats, like cork or plastic foam.

To Make the Sailboat

Cut the top part off the bottle about 2 to 3 inches from the bottom. The bottom part will become the boat. Cut the neck ring from the top of the bottle. Glue the ring in the center of the bottom of the boat. Let dry. Cut a sail from white paper. Cover both sides of the sail with clear packing tape to make it waterproof. Glue the sail to the straw. Let dry. Press some clay into the neck ring. Press the bottom end of the straw into the clay to mount the sail. Add decorations using permanent markers.

To Make Columbus's Ship

Cut the top part off the white dish-soap bottle, leaving the base about 4 inches tall. Cut around the edge of the bottle as shown. Use the hole punch to make portholes. Glue the toothpaste cap inside the bottom center of the ship. Paint the outside of the ship. Cut a tiny rail from the side of the berry basket. Glue the rail to the back of the ship. Cut a sail from bottle scraps and decorate with permanent markers. Glue the sail to a piece of dowel. Glue the end of the dowel inside the toothpaste cap. If it is not snug, wrap the end of the dowel in glue-soaked cotton to create a tight fit.

Windmill

Set this on your windowsill to welcome spring.

You Will Need:

- hole punch
- plastic dish-soap bottle
- paper scraps
- craft bead
- plastic lid or bottle in a different color
- metal paper fastener

1 Punch a hole in the top front of the bottle.

2 Cut doors, windows, and tulips from paper scraps, and glue them on the bottle.

3 Glue a small bead on the door for a doorknob.

4 Cut two strips from another bottle or lid to make the paddles. Punch a hole in the center of each paddle. Attach the two paddles to the windmill with the paper fastener.

More Ideas

Make two windmills, fill them with small pebbles, and use as bookends.

"Let's Party" Hat

A hat like this will put anyone in a party mood.

You Will Need:

- paper plate
- disposable bowl
- pencil
- sticker stars
- balloons
- chenille sticks
- ribbons
- hole punch

1 Set the paper plate right-side up. Place the bowl in the center, and trace around it with the pencil. Draw a second circle about ¾ inches in from the first circle. Cut out the smaller circle. Turn the plate over.

2 Spread glue around the edge of the opening. Set the bowl over the opening. Let the glue dry.

3 Decorate the hat with sticker stars. Blow a little air into the balloons, and knot them. Make chenille-stick coils by wrapping them around the pencil. Tie the balloons and coils with ribbon. Staple the decorations around the brim.

4 Cut long pieces of ribbons for ties. Punch a hole in the brim on each side of the hat. Attach the ribbons.

More Ideas

Use different-size containers for larger or smaller hats.

Use bottle caps to make hats for dolls. Glue paper circles underneath for the brims.

Teapot Tea-Bag Holder

It's teatime. This teapot is really a storage container for tea bags.

You Will Need:

- round container with plastic lid
- self-adhesive paper
- bottle cap
- construction paper
- fabric trim

1 Cover the outside of the container and lid with the self-adhesive paper.

2 Glue the bottle cap to the center of the lid. Cover the top of the cap with construction paper. Add trims.

3 Cut a strip of construction paper. Glue the two ends of the strip to the container to make the handle.

4 Roll a square of paper into a spout. Secure the rolled spout with tape. Cut four 1-inch slits around one end of the spout. Spread the tabs out, and glue the spout to the container. Use tape to help hold the spout in place while the glue dries. Trim the spout.

More Ideas

Cover the container with fabric scraps instead of paper for a textured design.

Berry-Basket Frame

Show off your latest school picture in this neat frame.

You Will Need:

- plastic berry basket
- pencil
- construction paper
- ribbon
- thin cardboard

1 Cut the bottom off the berry basket. Cut the center out, leaving a border.

2 Trace around the outside and the inside of the frame on construction paper. Cut the tracing out.

3 Weave ribbon into each side of the frame, if you wish. Glue the edges down on each end to secure the ribbon. Glue the basket frame to the construction-paper frame.

4 Trace around the outside of the frame on cardboard. Cut the cardboard tracing out. Glue the two sides and the bottom edge of the frame to the cardboard.

5 Cut a triangle shape from the cardboard, slightly shorter than the height of the frame. Bend the two sides of the triangle. Glue the flat part of the triangle to the back of the frame to make a stand. Slip your picture inside the frame through the opening at the top.

More Ideas

Add other decorations to your frame, such as sticker stars or tiny seashells.

Great Games

These hand-held games don't need batteries.

You Will Need:

- small margarine tubs with lids
- corrugated cardboard
- markers
- hole punch
- red craft beads
- plastic wrap
- bottle cap, round stickers, reinforcement rings
- small pompon
- clear packing tape
- thin ribbon

To Make the Apple Tree Game

Cut a 1½-inch band from the top of the tub. Trace around the bottom of the band on the corrugated cardboard twice. Cut out both circles. Trim the edges of one of the circles until it fits snugly inside the band. Remove the circle, and draw an apple tree with markers. Punch holes in the branches where apples should be. Press the other cardboard circle inside the plastic band, and glue in place. Put glue underneath the apple-tree circle, and press it to the bottom of the puzzle. Let dry. Add a red bead for each hole in the picture. Cut out the center of the lid so that you are left with only the rim. Cover the top of the puzzle with clear plastic wrap. Snap on the lid rim. Trim the excess wrap. See if you can shake all the "apples" in place.

To Make the Lion Skill Game

Glue the cap, open-side up, to the center bottom of the tub. Let the glue dry. Use the stickers to make a lion face. Drop the pompon into the container. Cut out the center portion from the lid, leaving an inch-wide rim. Cover the opening on both sides with clear packing tape. Punch holes three-quarters of the way around the rim. Tie ribbon through each hole to make a mane. Punch two holes, side by side, in the bottom edge of the lid. Thread a piece of ribbon through the holes and tie in a bow. Trim the edge of two round stickers. Stick one on each side of the mane for the ears. Snap the lid on over the face. Help the lion get a nose by getting the pompon into the cap.

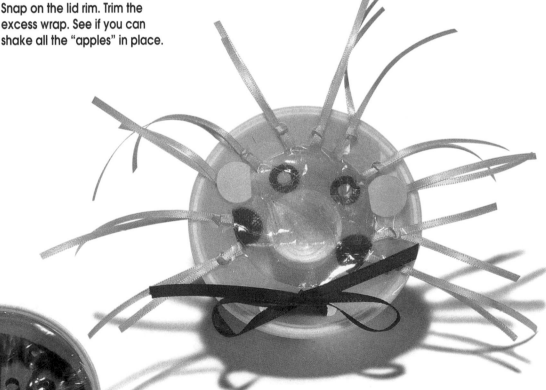

More Ideas

You might have another idea for a puzzle picture. You could make a face with holes for the eyes, nose, and mouth. How about a row of candles with holes for the flames?

Simplify the games by including only holes or a cap and a pompon, rather than drawing a picture.

13

...And More Games

Make these games, then challenge your skills.

You Will Need:

- milk jug
- hole punch
- chenille sticks
- paint and paintbrush
- string
- sponge
- medium-size plastic-foam balls
- pencil
- large plastic lids
- small pebbles
- plastic soda bottle
- round stickers or construction paper
- bottle cap
- pompon
- yarn
- plastic wiggle eyes

To Make the Toss-and-Catch Jug Game

Cut the top section off the milk jug. Punch holes around the cut edge of the catcher. Weave chenille sticks in and out of the holes all the way around the edge. Paint designs on the bottle. Let the paint dry. Cut a 2- to 3-foot length of string. Tie one end of the string around the neck of the bottle. Tie the sponge to the other end of the string. Hold onto the handle and try to catch the sponge in the catcher.

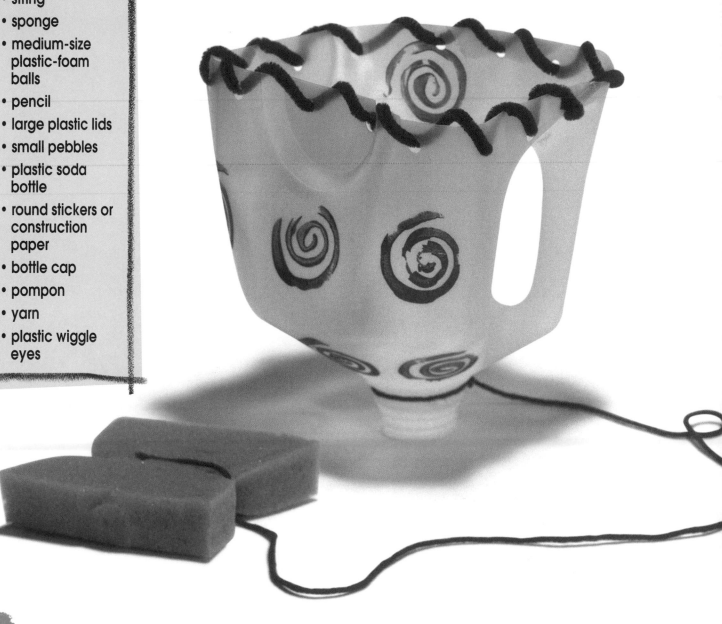

To Make the Wraparound Game

Paint the plastic-foam ball and let it dry. Cut a 2-foot piece of string. Poke a small hole in the ball with the point of the pencil. Fill the hole with glue, then use the pencil to push one end of the string into the ball. Let the glue dry. Cut the center from a large lid to make a ring. Tie the end of the string to the ring. Toss the ball into the air and try to get it through the ring. Keep going until the string is wrapped around the edge of the ring.

To Make the Bottle Clown Hoopla

Put some small pebbles in the bottom of the soda bottle to keep it from tipping over. Decorate the bottle with round stickers or construction paper. Firmly push and twist the plastic-foam ball onto the neck of the bottle. Press the cap into the head for a hat. Remove the cap, dip the edges in glue, then put it back on the head. Glue a pompon to the top. Add a yarn chin strap. Use stickers and the wiggle eyes to give the clown a face. Cut the center out of each lid so that you are left with the rims to use as hoops. Try to throw the rings over the clown.

More Ideas

Make the Toss-and-Catch Jug Game more challenging: the longer the string, the harder it is to play.

Have a friend make a Wraparound Game, too, and have a wraparound race.

15

Finger Soccer

This game goes anywhere.

You Will Need:

- green paint and paintbrush
- corrugated cardboard
- white correction pen
- plastic berry basket
- chenille sticks
- aluminum foil

1 Paint a rectangle of corrugated cardboard green. Use the white correction pen to add lines to the field.

2 Cut the berry basket in half to make the two goals. Place them at each end of the field.

3 Poke two holes in the cardboard on each side of the goals. Thread chenille sticks up through one hole, through the side of the goal, and down through the second hole. Twist the ends of the chenille sticks together to secure them.

4 Make a ball from aluminum foil. Your hand will be the soccer player for this game, using the middle finger and pointer for legs to kick the ball.

More Ideas

Take this in the car when you travel with a friend, brother, or sister.

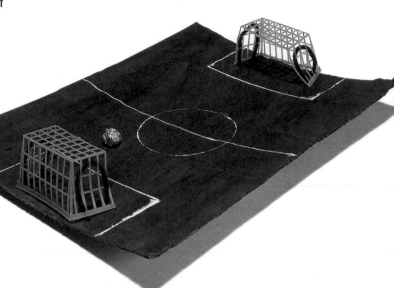

Disc Flyer

Play catch outside with this easy-to-make flyer.

You Will Need:

- large round bleach bottle
- construction paper

3 Hold the disc flyer between your thumb and index finger, and toss it to a friend.

More Ideas

Take this and the Sand Pail and Scoop on page 17 to the beach.

1 Cut the bottom from the bottle.

2 Cut small shapes from construction paper. Glue the shapes on the flyer to decorate it.

Sand Pail and Scoop

Build your sand castles with these handy beach toys.

You Will Need:

- two plastic milk jugs or large bleach bottles, one with a cap
- hole punch
- twine
- paint and paintbrush

1 To make the sand pail, cut the top off the milk jug. The bottom will become the pail.

2 Punch two holes on two opposite sides. Thread a length of twine through the holes. Knot them together to form a handle.

3 To make the scoop, leave the cap on the jug. Cut away the bottom of the jug and the two sides below the handle to form a giant scoop.

4 Decorate the pail and scoop with paints.

More Ideas

When you're heading to the beach, bring along clean plastic tubs of all sizes to make different sand shapes.

Garden-Variety Fun

Attract birds to your yard with an easy-to-make feeder and birdhouse.

You Will Need:

- gallon and half-gallon jugs
- colored plastic tape
- acrylic paints and paintbrush
- foam paint stamps
- self-adhesive paper
- aluminum pie pan
- metal paper fastener
- string
- empty seed packets
- hole punch
- clear packing tape
- sticks

To Make the Bottle Bird Feeder

Cut a large rectangle from the front of a gallon-size jug. Tape the edges. Use paint to decorate your feeder.

To Make the Plastic Watering Jug

Use the foam stampers to stamp a pretty design with paint on a milk jug. Add details using the paintbrush.

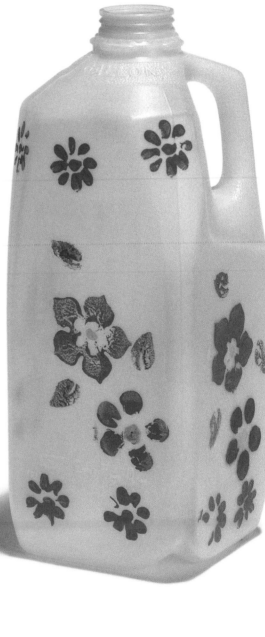

Then create the handy plant markers and watering jug for a cheerful garden.

To Make the Jug Birdhouse

Cut a hole on one side of a jug about 2 inches up from the bottom. The hole should be large enough to put your fist through. Cut shapes from the self-adhesive paper, and stick them on the side. Poke a small hole through the bottom of the jug and the center of the pie pan. Add more holes on the bottom of the pan, near the sides. Glue the bottom of the jug to the inside of the pan. Push a fastener through the holes in the center of the jug and pie pan. Tie a piece of string around the neck of the jug for a hanger. Put the cap on the jug.

To Make the Milk Jug Plant Markers

Cut a rectangular shape from the side of a milk jug. Cut the front from the packet of seeds you wish to mark, and glue the picture on the plastic rectangle. Punch a hole in the top and bottom of the marker. (This is easiest to do before the glue dries.) Cover the front and back with clear packing tape. Punch through the tape in the holes you've already made. Insert the stick through the holes.

More Ideas

Use permanent markers or self-adhesive paper to decorate the watering jug.

Make your own paint stampers by cutting simple shapes from a plastic-foam tray and gluing each shape to an empty thread spool.

Patchwork Purse and Hat

Wear your own designer accessories.

To Make the Purse

Cut lots of 2-inch squares from different fabrics. Cut the bottom part off the bleach bottle, just below the handle. Cover the bottom with glued fabric patches. Cover the top edge with plastic tape. Poke a hole on each side of the purse. Cut long pieces of ribbon. Thread the ends through the holes, and knot the ends to make a handle.

To Make the Hat

Cut the handle from the top of the bottle. Glue a patch of fabric over the two holes where the handle was removed. Cover the hat with glued fabric patches. Cover the cut edge with plastic tape. Glue the pompon in the spout. Poke a hole on each side of the hat. Cut four long pieces of ribbon. Tie the ends through each hole to make ties.

More Ideas

Use the hat design on page 11, and cover the hat with the same fabric scraps to match your purse.

20

Cardholder

This will come in hand-y when playing card games.

You Will Need:

- two lids from small margarine tubs
- metal paper fastener
- stickers

1 Poke a hole in the center of each lid.

2 Hold them together, print sides in, with the paper fastener.

3 Decorate the outsides with stickers.

4 Slip your playing cards in between the two lids.

More Ideas

Glue your favorite playing card from an old deck to your cardholder.

Nature Paperweight

Bring a bit of the outdoors to your desk.

You Will Need:

- small plastic soda bottle
- pencil
- cardboard
- green paint and paintbrush
- small pebbles
- dried flowers and leaves
- green yarn

1 Cut a dome from the bottom of the bottle.

2 Trace around the opening of the bottle on the cardboard. Cut the circle out, making it slightly larger.

3 Paint the circle green.

4 Glue pebbles, flowers, and leaves on the cardboard.

5 Glue the plastic bottle dome over the arrangement. Tie green yarn around the base of the paperweight.

More Ideas

Add tiny figures, such as deer or birds, to your scene.

Make several paperweights and give as gifts.

Mess Masters

This trash eater and toy tamer will help keep your room tidy.

You Will Need:

- gallon-size plastic bleach bottle
- yarn
- rickrack and other trims
- large plastic wiggle eyes
- pompon
- permanent marker
- milk jug or laundry detergent bottle
- construction paper

To Make the Garbage Gobbler

Cut the top part of the bleach bottle almost all the way off, leaving a hinge near the handle. (By pulling on the handle, the bottle should open and shut.) Glue tufts of yarn inside the spout for hair. Glue rickrack around the top and bottom of the opening to look like teeth. Glue on the wiggle eyes and a pompon nose. Add face details with permanent marker. Decorate the bottle with fabric trims.

To Make the Toy Stasher

Cut the top off the milk jug or detergent bottle, leaving the handle. Paint the bottle, or leave it the original color. Glue on a face made from cut paper.

More Ideas

Create other animal faces, such as a bear or a mouse. Use yarn to make fur.

Bottle Sculpture

Express yourself with this free-form work of art.

You Will Need:

- 2-liter plastic soda bottle
- old compact disc (CD)

1 Cut the spout from the bottle and save for another project.

2 Start cutting around the side of the bottle, going around and around so that you have a continuous strip of plastic.

3 Twist and bend the plastic strip into a sculpture, weaving the strip through itself to secure the loops of plastic.

4 Glue your work to the shiny side of the CD to display.

More Ideas

Set the sculpture near a window so the light will shine through the plastic and reflect off the CD.

Use two bottles of different colors to make a sculpture.

Cut geometric shapes from different-color containers, and glue them on the sculpture.

Mosaic Masterpiece

Arrange plastic squares to make a colorful creation.

You Will Need:

- plastic container scraps in different colors
- paper plate
- thin ribbon

1 Cut the plastic scraps into ½-inch squares.

2 Arrange the squares on the paper plate in a design or a picture. Glue the squares in place.

3 Cut a piece of thin ribbon to use as a hanger. Glue the ends to the back of the mosaic.

More Ideas

Use the squares to make a picture on a scrap of wood.

Use a colored paper plate for the base, or paint or color a plate with markers.

Wrap the plate in plastic wrap and use it to serve cookies. To clean it, just change the plastic-wrap covering.

Drum Set

Keep the beat while you keep secret stuff inside.

You Will Need:

- small, medium, and large plastic tubs with lids
- aluminum foil
- construction paper
- two metal paper fasteners
- chenille stick
- extra lid
- old compact disc (CD)

1 Cover the three tubs with aluminum foil. Cover their lids with glue and construction paper.

2 Poke a hole in one side of the two smaller tubs. Poke a hole through each side of the large tub at the top. Attach a smaller tub to each side of the large tub using a paper fastener.

3 Poke two holes through the side of the large tub. Thread the chenille stick through the two holes.

4 Cut two plastic circles from the extra lid to make the cymbals. Cover each cymbal with construction paper. Poke a hole in the center of each cymbal. Slide the cymbals onto the ends of the chenille stick. Trim off any excess. Fold the ends down and secure them with glue.

5 Snap the lids on all three drums. Glue the shiny side of the CD to the large drum to steady the set.

More Ideas

Write the name of your favorite music group on the large drum, or make up a name for your own group.

Desk Mates

Deck out your desk with these holders and helpers.

You Will Need:

- plastic dish-soap bottles
- plaster of Paris (follow the directions on the package)
- paint and paintbrush
- felt scraps
- sponge
- gallon-size plastic container
- yarn

To Make the Basic Holder

1 Cut off as much as necessary from the bottle to make the holder you want.

2 Fill the holder with plaster of Paris for a base. Let the plaster dry for an hour.

3 Paint the holder, and decorate with felt scraps. Glue felt underneath.

To Make the Letter Holder

Cut a ½-inch-wide slit out of each side of a bottle. Leave about 1 inch below each slit so there is a base at the bottom of the letter slit. Fill the bottom with plaster of Paris up to the slits.

To Make the Pencil Holder

Add about 1 inch of plaster of Paris to the bottom.

To Make the Stamp Sponge

Add about 1½ inches of plaster of Paris to the bottom. Cut a piece of sponge to fit in the top. Moisten the sponge as needed to wet your stamps.

To Make the Scrap Basket

Cut off the top portion of the gallon-size container. Decorate with felt and yarn.

More Ideas

Decorate the holders with photographs, pictures cut from greeting cards or wallpaper, or your own drawings.

Create more holders as you need them. How about a paper clip holder? Or one for pushpins?

Bottle Banks

Keep the lid on your savings.

You Will Need:

- 3-liter clear soda bottle with cap
- pink and black construction paper
- black chenille stick
- four film canisters
- large clear plastic bottle with wide neck and cap
- aluminum foil
- nuts, bolts, lids, bottle caps, and other items
- felt

To Make the Piggy Bank

Cover the end of the cap with a circle of pink paper. Glue two small black dots for the nostrils. Make eyes from the black construction paper. Glue them near the nose. Cut triangle-shaped ears from the pink paper. Pleat the bottoms. Glue the bottom of each ear to the head. Cut spots from the black and pink paper, and glue them on the body. Poke a hole in the bottom of the bottle. Wrap the black chenille stick around your finger to make a curly tail. Dip one end of the tail in glue and stick it in the hole. Cut a coin slot in the top of the pig. Glue paper to the bottom of the pig. Then glue the film canisters toward the front and back to create legs. Keep the pig upside down and undisturbed until the glue has dried.

To Make the Robot Money Guard

Cover the the cap of a large clear plastic bottle with aluminum foil. Make sure you can still screw the cap on and off the bottle. Give the robot facial features using nuts, bolts, and other items. Glue square panels of felt to the front and the back. Give the robot an array of buttons and switches using your caps and other objects.

More Ideas

Use other materials to make your favorite animals or characters. You could use craft feathers to make a bird or cotton balls to make a rabbit.

Jingle Ghosts

Are those ghosts ringing?

You Will Need:

- plastic milk jug
- hole punch
- thread
- jingle bells

1 Cut ghost shapes from the sides of the milk jug.

2 Punch eyeholes in the head of each ghost.

3 Poke a small hole in the top of each ghost. Tie a loop of thread through each hole to make a hanger. Poke a small hole in the bottom of each ghost. Thread a jingle bell onto a piece of thread, and tie the thread to the ghost.

More Ideas

Hang the ghosts in a breezy place to hear the bells jingle.

Make shapes for other holidays, such as Christmas or Independence Day.

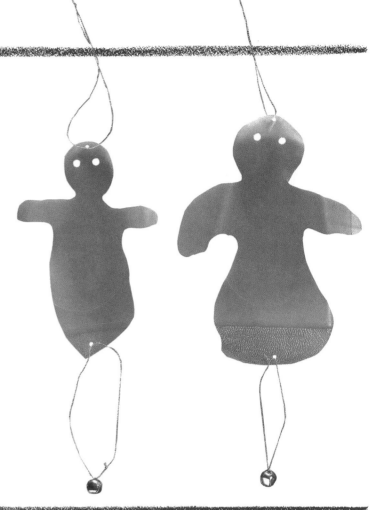

Pincushion

This is just what a sewer needs.

You Will Need:

- margarine tub with lid
- cotton balls
- fabric
- rickrack, ribbon, and other trims

1 Cut the center from the lid, leaving the narrow rim around the outside.

2 Stuff the tub with cotton balls.

3 Squeeze glue around the top edge of the tub. Lay a piece of fabric over the top of the tub, and snap the lid rim over the fabric to secure it. Trim off the excess fabric around the outside.

4 Decorate with rickrack and other trims.

More Ideas

Pincushions don't have to be square. Look for rectangular tubs with lids.

Bathroom Basketries

Scrub-a-dub-dub! Someone you know would like these baskets to store soap and such.

You Will Need:

- round plastic food containers
- fabric
- ruler
- pencil
- ribbon
- plastic dish-soap bottle
- paper
- sponge
- permanent marker
- hole punch
- two long shoelaces

To Make the Soap Basket

Place a plastic container in the center of the fabric. Measure the height of the container. Add about 1½ inches to this measurement. Measure the fabric starting from the bottom of the container until you reach the total measurement you want. Make small marks on the fabric with the pencil, going all the way around the container. (You should see a circle forming.) Cut the circle out. Squeeze glue around the inside rim of the container. Place the container in the center of the fabric. Pull the fabric up around the container and press the edges into the glue. Work the fabric evenly around the rim. Let the glue dry. Tie a ribbon around the outside.

To Make the Toothy Toothbrush Holder

Cut the top part off the dish-soap bottle. Cut rounded sections out of the front and the back of the bottle so that the sides look like the roots of a tooth. Poke a few holes in the bottom for drainage. Press a piece of scrap paper into the bottom of the bottle to make a pattern. Trim off the excess paper from the pattern so that it fits in the bottom. Use the pattern to cut a piece of sponge. Place the sponge in the bottom of the holder. Write a name with permanent marker on the front.

To Make the Shower Caddy

Poke three holes in the bottom of each container. Poke or punch a hole on the top and bottom of opposite sides of each container. Knot the end of one shoelace. Thread the other end in the bottom hole of one container and out the top hole on the same side. Pull the lace tight, then add the second container, and then the third. Do the same thing with the other shoelace on the opposite sides. Arrange the containers so they are evenly spaced and hang straight. Tie the two loose ends of the laces together at the top to create a hanger. Hang this caddy over the shower fixture to hold bath and shower supplies.

More Ideas

Turn the soap basket into a planter by lining it with an identical container. It could also make a terrific dresser catchall for coins, jewelry, or small toys.

Tom

Money-Holder Necklace

This necklace is perfect for keeping track of your lunch money.

You Will Need:

- film canister
- yarn
- pencil with a point
- craft beads
- rickrack or other trims

1 Poke a tiny hole in the center of the lid.

2 Cut a 2-foot piece of yarn. Thread the two ends of the yarn down from the top through the hole in the lid. (You may need a pencil to help push the ends through.) Knot the two ends together, and pull the knot up tight against the inside of the lid.

3 Thread craft beads onto the double strand of yarn outside the lid. Slide the beads down.

4 Decorate the outside of the canister with rickrack or other trims. Wear the necklace around your neck so your money is there when you need it.

More Ideas

Make the holder without the yarn necklace. Store paper clips inside.

Raggedy Crayon Doll

This little helper can hold an armful.

You Will Need:

- plastic dish-soap bottle
- hole punch
- yarn
- felt
- two small buttons
- rickrack and other trims

1 Cut off the top half of the bottle, leaving an oval-shaped piece attached to the back.

2 Punch holes around the head. Cut pieces of yarn. Tie two pieces through each hole to make the hair.

3 Cut a triangle nose from felt. Glue the nose, two button eyes, and a yarn smile to the head.

4 Cut two arms from felt. Cut two hands, and glue one to the end of each arm. Glue an arm on each side.

5 Decorate with rickrack and other trims.

More Ideas

Use curling ribbon to make hair or plastic wiggle eyes instead of buttons.

Desk Aquarium

Keep these carefree fish on your desk or shelf.

You Will Need:

- 3-liter soda bottle
- masking tape
- colored plastic tape
- 42-ounce oatmeal container
- black poster paint and paintbrush
- light-colored construction paper
- markers
- string
- pencil
- corrugated cardboard
- felt
- green chenille sticks

1 Cut the bottle in half. Fold masking tape over the bottom edge to create a better gluing surface. Wrap colored plastic tape around the outside edge to cover the masking tape.

2 Cut a 2½-inch-tall piece from the bottom of the oatmeal container. Paint it black. Turn the bottom half of the bottle upside down to form the aquarium. Put some strips of masking tape over the dome to create a better gluing surface. Glue the black box over the top of the dome.

3 Fold the construction paper in half. Draw some fish. Cut them out so that you have two sides for each fish. Color the fish on both sides.

4 Cut pieces of string. Glue the two sides of each fish together with the end of a string in between. Use masking tape to tape the other end of each string inside the dome so the fish hang down.

5 Trace around the open end of the aquarium on the cardboard. Cut the circle out, and cover it with felt. Shape some seaweed plants out of the chenille sticks. Glue the seaweed to the felt-covered cardboard. Glue the bottle in place over the cardboard with the fish hanging down.

More Ideas

Make smaller aquariums from smaller bottles.

Add old aquarium decorations, such as a diver or a treasure chest. Glue small pebbles on the bottom.

Bookend Friends

Turn a pair of bottles into some very unusual bookends.

You Will Need:

- two identical laundry detergent bottles with handles
- felt
- plastic wiggle eyes
- white sequins
- ribbons and trims
- craft feathers
- large pompons

To Make the Elephants

The handle will form the trunk. Cover the bottle with felt. Glue two wiggle eyes above each trunk. Glue on sequins for toe nails. Cut ears from felt, and glue in place. Decorate the cap of each bottle to look like a hat.

To Make the Birds

Glue a long triangle of felt over each handle for a beak. Glue two wiggle eyes on the handle. Glue lots of feathers on each side of the bottles for wings. Glue a large pompon in the spout along with three or four feathers.

More Ideas

Put stones in the bookends to give them extra weight.

What other animal could you make? A lion with a yarn mane? A peacock with construction-paper feathers?

YOLEN ~ STEMPLE   COLOR ME A RHYME   WORDSONG ~ BOYDS MILLS PRESS

LIGHT, SHADOWS, AND MIRRORS   Highlights

FASCINATING FOOD   Highlights

Jane Yolen's Mother Goose Songbook   Yolen / Stemple / Hoffman   Caroline House • Boyds Mills Press

LARRICK / O'NEILL   TO THE MOON AND BACK

"What a Doll" Telephone Pal

Stand this friend next to the phone, and those important numbers will always be handy.

You Will Need:

- plastic dish-soap bottle
- 3-inch plastic-foam ball
- colored map pins
- yarn
- ribbon and trims
- felt scraps
- black permanent marker

1 Remove the cap from the bottle. Firmly push and twist the plastic-foam ball over the neck of the bottle.

2 Push the map pins into the front of the ball to create a face. Glue yarn bits to the head. Attach a bow to the hair with a map pin.

3 Glue on rows of trim and ribbon to decorate the dress. Glue a bow at the neck.

4 Cut arms and hands from the felt scraps. Glue a hand to each arm. Decorate with trim. Glue an arm on each side of the body, then glue the two hands together.

5 Use the black marker to write important phone numbers on the dress.

More Ideas

Add a loop of colored tape to hold a pen or a pencil to the doll.

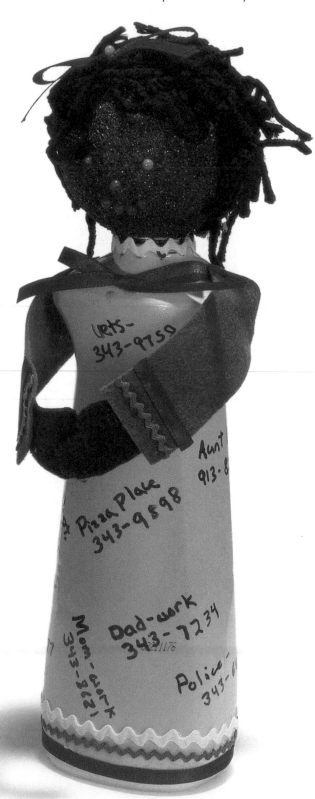

Hanging Planter

Here's a simple hanging basket to hold a favorite plant.

You Will Need:

- large plastic bottle
- paint and paintbrush
- hole punch
- twine

1 Cut off the bottom half of the plastic bottle.

2 Decorate the planter with paint.

3 Punch three evenly spaced holes around the rim.

4 Cut three 18-inch pieces of twine. Knot the three pieces together at one end.

5 Thread one length of twine through each of the three holes. Tie the ends of the twine together underneath the planter.

More Ideas

Decorate your planter with flower stickers instead of paint.

Add small pebbles to the bottom of your planter if you're planting seeds or transplanting a plant.

Bottle Bracelets

Wear this jewelry with your favorite outfit, or give as a gift.

You Will Need:

- small plastic soda bottle
- rickrack or other fabric trims
- small beads

1 Cut the spout off the bottle. Cut around the bottle to make 1-inch bands. Use scissors to even out the edges.

2 Glue trims and beads around each band.

More Ideas

Try covering a bracelet with yarn, either by wrapping yarn around the bracelet or gluing pieces of yarn across the band lengthwise.

Use old jewelry pieces to trim a bracelet.

How about decorating with nail polish?

Holiday Candy Cups

Make these delightful candy-cup favors for your holiday party.

You Will Need:

- small plastic bottles and containers
- pen
- white and green tissue paper
- plastic wiggle eyes
- pompons
- chenille stick
- ribbons and trims
- red nail polish
- yarn
- craft beads, glitter, sequins, sticker stars, sparkle stems
- felt
- cotton swab
- hole punch
- marker

To Make the Basic Candy Container

1 Cut off the top of the container. Cut away part of the back and sides, leaving the front and a cup, about 1½ to 3 inches tall, at the bottom.

2 Use the pen to sketch the shape you want. Cut around the shape so that it sticks up from the candy cup.

To Make the Shamrock Candy Cup

Cover the shamrock shape with glued-on bits of crumpled green tissue paper. Glue on wiggle eyes, a pompon nose, and a chenille-stick smile. Glue a bow on the stem.

To Make the Valentine Candy Cup

Use a pink or white container. Paint the heart with red nail polish. Decorate the heart with glued-on bits of white tissue paper. Glue trims around the container. Tie pink and red ribbons around the container in a bow.

To Make the Chocolate Bunny Candy Cup

Use a brown container. Glue wiggle eyes and a pink pompon nose on the bunny head. Knot two pieces of pink ribbon or yarn together in the center, and glue them under the nose for whiskers. Glue trims around the container. Glue a big bow at the neck.

To Make the Christmas Tree Candy Cup

Cover the tree shape with glued-on bits of green yarn. Decorate the tree with beads, sequins, sparkle stems, and sticker stars. Cut a stand from felt. Glue a piece of trim across the felt. Glue the stand under the tree.

To Make the Dreidel Candy Cup

Cover the dreidel shape with glue, then blue glitter. Add one of the four Hebrew letters found on a dreidel using pieces of silver sparkle stem. Cut off one end of a cotton swab. Dip the cotton in glue, then in silver glitter to make a handle. Tape the handle to the back of the dreidel shape.

To Make the Ghost Candy Cup

Use a white or opaque container. Punch two small holes for eyes. Punch several small overlapping holes to make a larger hole for the mouth. Punch a hole in one hand. Use a marker to color a wooden bead for a pumpkin. Draw on a jack-o'-lantern face. Glue a piece of green chenille stick in the hole in the bead for a stem. Attach the stem to the ghost's hand.

More Ideas

Line the cups with small squares of tissue paper in holiday colors.

Tillie the Turkey Centerpiece

This turkey will be the talk of your Thanksgiving table.

You Will Need:

- gallon milk jug
- construction paper
- red plastic cup
- red chenille stick

1 Cut around the handle portion of the milk jug to remove it. (Do not cut off the neck of the jug.)

2 Glue cut-paper eyes and a beak to the cup. Twist the chenille stick around your finger to make the turkey's wattle. Glue the wattle to one side of the beak. Glue the head over the neck of the jug.

3 Cut lots of paper feathers, and glue them on the jug.

4 Make a fan of large, colorful paper feathers for the tail. Staple the feathers together. Glue the tail to the back.

More Ideas

Fill the jug with dried or artificial flowers.

Holiday Noisemaker

Give this a shake and celebrate the new year or Purim.

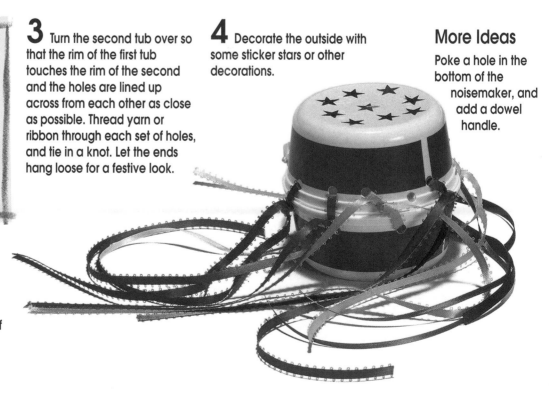

You Will Need:

- hole punch
- two identical margarine tubs
- small pebbles
- ribbon or yarn
- sticker stars

1 Punch eight holes, evenly spaced, around the rims of both tubs.

2 Put some pebbles in one of the tubs.

3 Turn the second tub over so that the rim of the first tub touches the rim of the second and the holes are lined up across from each other as close as possible. Thread yarn or ribbon through each set of holes, and tie in a knot. Let the ends hang loose for a festive look.

4 Decorate the outside with some sticker stars or other decorations.

More Ideas

Poke a hole in the bottom of the noisemaker, and add a dowel handle.

Clown Note Holder

This little friend holds messages that you can change in a snap.

You Will Need:

- construction paper
- 16-ounce clear plastic bottle
- paint and paintbrush
- felt, fabric, yarn, ribbon, and other trims
- medium-size plastic-foam ball
- pompons
- old sock
- old compact disc (CD)
- spring-type clothespin
- string
- markers

1 Cut a heart shape from paper. Tape it to the bottom of the bottle. Paint the bottle around the heart. Let the paint dry. Remove the paper to reveal the unpainted heart shape.

2 Cut arms, feet, and a collar from felt or paper. Glue them in place. Decorate the body using felt, ribbon, and other trims.

3 Twist the plastic-foam ball onto the bottleneck. Use yarn and trims to give the clown a face and hair.

4 Cut the cuff from the sock to use as a hat. Tie off the open end of the hat with yarn or ribbon. Glue the bottom of the clown to a CD.

5 Tie the clothespin to one end of a piece of string. Color the clothespin with markers. Attach a note to the clothespin. Lower the clothespin and note down inside the body so that you can read the note through the heart. Secure the string by twisting the head over it, leaving the excess string hanging down in back of the clown.

More Ideas

You can create other characters, such as a witch with a felt cape or a rabbit with floppy felt ears.

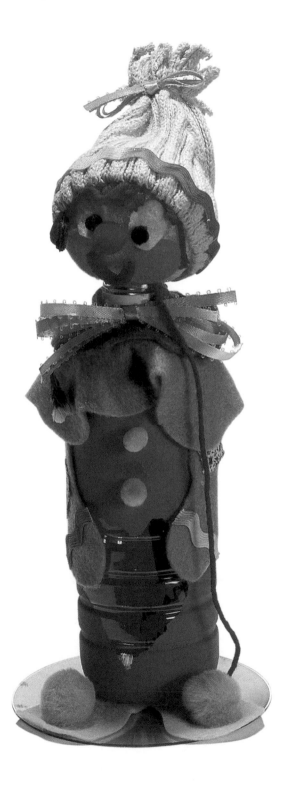

A Bunch of Baskets

A tiskit, a tasket, you'll love these springtime baskets.

You Will Need:

- construction paper
- pencil
- large and small plastic bottles and tubs
- thin cardboard
- hole punch
- metal paper fasteners
- pompons
- plastic scraps
- pen
- felt
- plastic wiggle eyes
- chenille sticks
- ribbons and trims

To Make the Confetti Basket

Cut narrow 2-inch strips of construction paper. Curl each strip around a pencil. Cover a margarine tub with the curled strips. Cut a handle from thin cardboard. Cover both sides with construction paper. Glue the two ends of the handle in place. Decorate the handle with pretty ribbons.

To Make the Jumbo Basket

Cut a bleach bottle in half. Cut a 1-inch strip from around the top of the bottle to use as a handle. Scallop the edges of the strip. Cut slits around the edge of the basket. Bend the tabs outward. Punch a hole in each end of the handle and on each side of the basket. Use paper fasteners to attach the handle. Decorate the basket with glued-on cut-paper flowers with tiny pompon centers.

To Make the Mini Basket

Use a small margarine tub with a pattern on the outside. Cut a handle from around another container. Punch a hole on each side of the basket and in each end of the handle. Attach the handle to the basket using paper fasteners. Cut a flower and leaves from plastic scraps. Punch a hole in the center of the flower and in the end of each leaf. Punch a hole in the handle, and attach the flower and leaves with a paper fastener.

To Make the Bunny Basket

Use the pen to sketch the head of a rabbit in the top portion of one corner of a milk jug. Cut around the head. Cut ear liners from pink felt or paper, and glue them in place. Glue on wiggle eyes, a pompon nose, and chenille-stick whiskers. Glue a big bow at the neck. Add trim around the edge of the basket.

More Ideas

Fill the baskets with paper grass or squares of colorful tissue paper and some Easter goodies.

Pedestal Snack Bowls

When you're ready for a party, fill these dishes with your favorite treats.

You Will Need:

- round plastic bottles or containers
- metal paper fasteners
- plastic cup or margarine tub
- permanent markers
- colored plastic tape

To Make the Basic Bowl

Choose the size bowl you want to make. Poke a hole in the bottom of the bowl and the base. Join them together, bottom to bottom, using a paper fastener.

More Ideas

For your party, decorate your balloons in the same color as your bowls. Use streamers that match.

To Make the Small Bowl

Use a margarine tub or other container for the bowl. Cut a plastic cup in half, and use the bottom part for your pedestal. Color with markers.

To Make the Large Bowl

Cut off the top portion of a bottle, and use the bottom for the bowl. Cut a scalloped edge around the bowl. Use a margarine tub for your base. Decorate the pedestal using strips of colored plastic tape or permanent markers.

Jack-o'-Lantern Party Favor

Fill this funny face with Halloween goodies.

You Will Need:

- pencil
- margarine tub with lid
- orange, green, and black construction paper
- hole punch
- green chenille stick

1 Trace around the lid of the container on the orange paper. Cut the circle out. Glue the circle to the lid. Stand the container on edge.

2 Cut a face and stem for the pumpkin, and glue them in place.

3 Poke two holes through the top edge of the pumpkin. Push the ends of the chenille stick through the holes to form a handle. Twist the two ends of the chenille stick together inside the pumpkin.

More Ideas

Make a bunch of these jack-o'-lanterns, and fasten them to fishing line. Hang in a window or a doorway.

Tea-Bag Caddy

This little teapot is perfect for a wet tea bag.

You Will Need:

- plastic dish-soap bottle
- pencil
- nontoxic permanent markers

1 Cut away the top part of the bottle.

2 Sketch the handle of the teapot on one side of the bottle and the spout on the other. Sketch the lid between the spout and the handle. Cut away the sides of the bottle, leaving the lid, spout, and handle.

3 Fold the parts of the teapot out and down on each side.

4 Use the markers to decorate the caddy.

More Ideas

If you're giving this to someone as a gift, you might want to write the person's name on the bottom of the caddy.

Hanging Creatures

These wacky animals will brighten your home.

You Will Need:

- plastic dish-soap bottle
- hole punch
- twine
- paint and paintbrush
- plastic scraps
- metal paper fasteners
- plastic wiggle eyes

To Make the Basic Planter

1 Cut an opening large enough to put a plant in one side of the bottle.

2 Punch a hole on each side of the opening. Thread twine through each hole. Tie a knot in each end to make a hanger. Decorate the bottle with paint.

To Make the Bird

Cut wings and a tail from the plastic scraps. Punch a hole in the wings, tail, and body. Attach the wings and tail to the body with paper fasteners. Glue wiggle eyes near the spout.

To Make the Fish

Cut fins and a tail from the plastic scraps. Punch a hole in the fins, tail, and body. Attach the fins and tail to the body with fasteners. Glue wiggle eyes to the sides of the bottle.

More Ideas

Add gravel to the bottom of the planters for drainage, then add dirt and some seeds or a plant.

Make a school of fish or a flock of birds to hang outside.

Make smaller creatures using travel-size bottles.

Title Index

Subject Index